PRAYERS
FROM A
WOMAN'S
HEART

PRAYERS
FROM A
WOMAN'S
HEART

Judith Mattison

Illustrations by
Audrey F. Teeple

Augsburg Publishing House

Minneapolis   Minnesota

PRAYERS FROM A WOMAN'S HEART

Manufactured in the United States of America

for

Char and Karen
Shirley and Carol
Faith and *Martha*

CONTENTS

PRAYERS FOR FEELINGS

PRAYERS FOR FAITH

A WORD
ABOUT
PRAYER

Prayer is like conversation. If I know another person, know her as a considerate and open friend, I have no trouble talking with her. Feelings and thoughts easily convert into words for a lively conversation. It's different when I don't know the other person well. I may be formal, stilted, afraid. The words don't come.

God has come to me as a friend in Jesus Christ. He shows me his love in countless ways and places. I know him as understanding, loving, forgiving, wise and powerful. I know I can count on his love, even when I am plagued by fears and feelings of complaint.

Prayer is not only *like* conversation: it is conversation with God. I often pray when I am active—driving the car, working at home, walking the aisles of the supermarket. My prayers cannot be confined to nightly ritual or Sunday worship. Yet I find that I need both—open conversations with God in the middle of a busy day, and a more disciplined prayer life at set times and in Sunday worship. Formal times of prayer can prepare me for prayer in the midst of life and its many surprises.

Always, whether formal or informal, prayer for me is especially significant because it is a tangible expression of my dependence on God. Whether I am on my knees in church or standing over the kitchen sink, prayers express my need for God and his love. Awareness of the exciting possibilities and opportunities of living prompt me to thank God for life. My deep feelings of sorrow and despair over my failings move me to search for a deeper relationship with God.

I am learning not to worry about the language of my prayers. Fumbling around for the "right" words gets in the way of being myself in his presence. God hears. He knows the sadness of my breaking heart, and the exuberance of happiest moments. God is my best listener. I know I can trust him, and that his power will break through to give me the need of the moment—more faith, understanding, forgiveness, or love.

These prayers are some of my conversations with God. I hope they suggest thoughts for personal prayer, and serve to strengthen your relationship with God and love for others and for life.

9

THE
CHILDREN
ARE FOREVER
NEEDING ME

Wet mittens,
four scarves,
snow-filled boots,
soaked socks,
    and a floor ruined with dirty water.
    "Help me, Mom. I can't get my hood untied."

Help *me*, Lord!
    I can't get my work done.
    The children are forever needing my help.

Oh, Lord, I'm sorry.
    I am glad that at this time in my life
        I feel very needed.
    I am a very important person.
        Children reinforce us so much
        while they are still young
        and in need of our protection.

I will need your direction
    when my children grow older
    and I begin to change my life patterns.
I will need to be reminded of the diverse ways
    one can love and serve and feel important
    to the lives of others—that there will be others
    who need me outside my family circle.

Until then,
    forgive me for my lapses of vision
    as I live day to day.
This is certainly a very fulfilling
    time of life for me.
I am so wanted, so needed.
It is good.

MY
BOY
LOVES
LIFE

What a wonderful little boy he is!
    He loves life—
        sand,
        snow,
        books,
        and music,
        anger,
        teasing,
        hugs,
        and laughter.
    He rejoices in it all!
    He lifts my spirits to a beautiful vista
        where living becomes
        adventure.

How I love this dear child of yours.
   Thank you for giving him to us.
   We will try to care for all his needs—
      to feed his curiosity
      to stretch his sensitivity
      to discipline his self-will
      to love him and love him and
      to allow him to be.
The responsibility is so great!
   But thank you for this wonderful experience!

I NEED
SOLITUDE

God, am I selfish to want solitude?
   David could go into the hills,
      to think,
      to search his soul,
      to reorder his life.
I need that sanctuary too, God.

I love my family.
I enjoy caring for them.
But sometimes I want to get away from
    the agitation of our lives,
    the harried mornings,
    the struggle to be a good listener to all of them
    and the demands of keeping
    a home moving smoothly.
I'd like to stand back and survey my family drawing,
    to reassess the shadings of individuality
    and the bold strokes of love.
I would be content to walk among trees
    rather than among crowds for just awhile.
        (How I appreciate your birch and pine
        and the quiet, soothing sounds they sing.)
I would be most grateful for a moment apart.
But make me also creative, Lord.
    Help me to see the possibilities for organization
        and to plan my time so I have quiet moments.
    Let me order my activity
        so that I best fulfill
        your purpose and my capabilities.
    Refresh my outlook.
    Renew my soul.

LET
MY
CHILDREN
GROW

Father, my heart and my stomach are sparring
    as I watch my boy leave
        for his first day of school.
    I must trust another person
        to be responsible for him.
I feel somehow empty now.
    I cried when he first
        crossed the alley all by himself.
    Tears are trailing my face now, too.
    It is hard to allow my child
        his birthright of independence.

Watch him, Lord.
  Every day, every curious moment
    is important to him.
  Help me understand that no teacher
    can be all things to all children.
  It is good for him to learn to adjust
    to new personalities,
    different rules,
    and a world of variation.
Help me to see my mission, too.
  As his mother, I am a most influential
    example and teacher.
  The most important lesson he can learn is to love.
Help me teach him the real meaning of love
  revealed in Jesus—
  and help me to trust his teachers.

WHAT
I NEED
IS A MOTHER

"What I need is a mother."
  The teenage girl, poring over a rack of clothes
    at the store, said the words.
  But I had been thinking them for days,
    "What I need is my mother."
I wanted someone to comfort me
  to advise me
  to tell me it's all right
  to say I love you
  to take my problems and solve them for me.
Being a mature adult is such a long, lasting experience.
  Sometimes it is overtaxing.

How good it would feel to slip back
    into the undemanding role of dependent child.
We experience youthful yearnings to grow up,
    only to have adult fantasies of
        the beauty of being a child again.
Help me Jesus,
    to accept my role, my responsibility, my choice.
Help me to see it as an opportunity
    and to realize that someday I may wish I had
    the mental or physical prowess of these adult years.
Help me to be that comforting mother
    my children need.
And help me to sense
    the tenor of our relationship, Jesus—
    yours and mine:
    that you are my comfort and my confidant,
    that you accept me and help me,
    that in a tenderness
        which surpasses a mother's love,
        you love me.
    Thank you, Lord.

GIVE
ME
EARPLUGS,
LORD

Give me earplugs, Lord.
The noise!
The noise of motherhood is just
   too much sometimes!
   The television is blaring.
   The boys are wrestling
     or pulling those toys
     with bells, bells, bells.
   The exhaust fan is running in the kitchen.
   Even the frying hamburgers are noisy!
I can't stand it!

This is what motherhood can be:
    whining children,
    gadgets that whirr and clank and break,
    a teenager "laying rubber" at the corner,
    and the sound of my grating voice
        repeating the same unheard
        usually unnecessary commands
        over and over
        in vain hope of obedience.
I think I need to get away from it all, Lord.
I'd like to take a trip,
    but I'd be satisfied with a locked bathroom
    if someone wouldn't be pounding on the door
        to tell me his latest adventure
        or to tattle on a neighbor.
    Right now I'd settle for my head
        in a drawer!
That's funny!
I can see me with my head in a drawer!
Well, if I can laugh, I can survive.
I'm sorry I complained, Lord.
    I'm sure you understand how I feel.
Thank goodness you are always listening
    and you don't plead for earplugs!

WE ARE GRATEFUL FOR GRANDPARENTS

We are grateful for grandparents, Lord.
> Theirs is a special place in the lives of the young.
> Often they are the ones who simply love
>> making few demands,
>> accepting,
>> and delighted by the spontaneity of children.
> They broaden the child's view
>> to see beyond a world of playmates and parents
>> to a world of other days past.
> They can show a child the value of unstructured
>> hours and a slower pace of life.
> A child learns to be more sympathetic and patient
>> when "Grandpa is tired" or
>> "Grandma's house is too small."

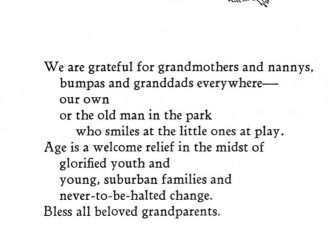

We are grateful for grandmothers and nannys,
    bumpas and granddads everywhere—
    our own
    or the old man in the park
        who smiles at the little ones at play.
Age is a welcome relief in the midst of
    glorified youth and
    young, suburban families and
    never-to-be-halted change.
Bless all beloved grandparents.

LORD,
I'M
TIRED

Lord, I am so terribly tired.
I am exhausted
   driving cars full of children
   ironing basketsful of clothes
   scheduling days full of demands
   fixing separate meals for family members
      all on the move
      in different directions.
This is today's family life.
Today's family must be free
   to go to new fields of learning
   where every person develops individually
   where the home becomes a haven
      not of sameness in personalities and interests
      nor of unimaginative togetherness
   but a haven
      where each person's uniqueness
      is cherished and encouraged
      in an intimate, tender way.

But Lord, I'm worn out!
   Where is my uniqueness?
   When do I get my opportunity for developing
      something besides fatigue or grocery lists?
Being a martyr doesn't work, Lord.
   I am not pacified by thinking that
      my family is my career,
      my extension of myself.
      The thought of their progress and their growth
      through my efforts does not always console me.
   The idea of being faced someday with an empty
         house
      is not always foreboding—
      it's appealing!
I'm sorry Lord, to complain so.
   I do feel taken advantage of.
   I feel fragmented by my family's demands.
   I haven't run across a creative approach
         to my routine
      since I used floral clay
      to repair my favorite planter—
      and then the plant died!
Please forgive my short-sighted view of this life.
Please revitalize me a bit
   so that I can create some adventure
   while I accept my responsibility—
      not so much as dutiful martyr
      but more as a loving mother.
I know you understand, Lord.
   I'm discouraged because I'm so terribly tired.
Help me.

HELP
ME
UNDERSTAND
MY HUSBAND

Help me Lord, to understand my husband.
Help me to glory in the differences:
    his optimism, my seriousness,
    his need to work, my need to feel,
    his need for quiet, my need to talk.
Let me appreciate the contrast—
    whether it is defined by our culture or
    innate in our souls or
    the result of the way we have
        learned to live together.

Help me allow him to be—
    to protect me, if he needs to
    to love me, for he does!
    to go away from me
        for a change of pace
        on the golf course or at a political meeting.
Give to my voice
    a song of thanks
        for his concern and his providing,
    a melody of praise
        which lifts his confidence
        and sustains his pride.
Let me sing to your creative power
    in making woman and man.
    For in loving him,
        I am loving you.

I WANT
TO BE FAIR

"You're wrong!" my child flails at me.
    And I shake within my fingertips,
I queaze inside my whole frame.
    For he will not cease to say,
        "You're wrong."
Perhaps I am wrong.
God, am I?
    I want to listen
    I want to be fair
    But I am used to being right!
       'You're wrong."

This stewardship, this care of children
    changes from protection
        to liberation
    and now they will not listen anymore.
    My children do not listen!
        (Whose children? Your children.)
Control this surge within me
    to reject the words he says
    when it is his tone of voice I despise.
Give me confidence in the fact
    that he must manifest your love
        in a different world from mine
    so it will be revealed differently—
        but it will still be you.
Help me guide
    but let me give him his birthright in Christ—
        the right to be an individual.

HELP
US TO
GROW
OLD

I watch the aging people—those who are nearly old.
It's hard, Jesus,
    to perform less adequately,
    to be subject to the will of more vigorous offspring.
    to try to achieve
    and be dashed against the reality that
        grandmothers get out of practice
        when they don't bake often,
        uncles and grandfathers can't always
        run during a baseball game,
        fathers shouldn't wrestle anymore,
        mothers can't understand the homework.

It's hard, Jesus,
   because we throw away
      old typewriters and clothes and cars,
   and we don't want to be human cast-offs.
   We don't want to be thrown away!
   We need to be loved.
Love us, Jesus.
   Help us rejoice in change—
      and make the best use of our waning skills
      and our added maturity.
   Help us love those who feel unneeded.
   Help us find and tap
      their strength of experience
      and their need to reminisce.
Love us, Jesus—
   healthy, vigorous, old, changing, weak sinners.
Love us—always, Lord.

THANK
YOU FOR
THE LOVE
OF FRIENDS

Dear God, I walked through the door,
   saw her coming,
   and I felt good.
   I felt glad.
There is a beautiful aura to friendships,
   a warm, close feeling one has
      when one is in harmony with another.
You have given us friends to keep us living.
   Sympathy, they say, is necessary
      to renew the spirit.
      Thank you for the sympathy of friends.
   Honesty builds strength and makes
      growing possible.
      Thank you for their honesty.
   Love takes many forms and endures.

Thank you for their love
   in a last minute offer to babysit
     when I have a chance to get away;
   in a phone call offering to bring
     dessert when she knew I was lonesome;
   in a bolstering of my spirit by saying,
     "Well done,";
   in a reassuring hand, reaching to squeeze
     mine among the crowd.
Thank you for the love of friends
   akin to the love of Christ,
   which surpasses all understanding
   and gives us reason to live.
God, bless my friends.

BLESS
THIS
NEW
MOTHER

My prayer is for a new mother.
Make her delivery as beautiful
   as only hard work and new life can be.
      Give her courage.
But also give her
   your love and comfort and strength
      in the days that follow.
   She will need the understanding
      of a loving husband
         to help her through the tiring nights.

She will need kindness
    and encouragement from friends
    to help her adjust to the demands of a newborn
    and the changes in her lifestyle.
And she surely will have
    the most glorious opportunity
    to experience the love of God in her life
    as she gives to this baby in the measure
    that only mothering can possess.
Thank you for giving women
    this marvelous possibility
    for sharing your love and patience
        through new life
        and growing children.
Send your Holy Spirit to show this special
    new mother how blessed she is
        in these precious,
        if trying days.

MAKE
ME A
GOOD
LISTENER

Dear God, I know this neighbor needs a listener.
   She has so many problems with her husband
   and her children.
We all need to share our problems.
   We talk it over, re-sort our ideas,
   talk some more, clarify feelings, and
   soon we begin to find our way.

But Father, I feel so inadequate.
   This problem is too great.
   It is too complex for her
      and too difficult for me.
I will pray for her.
I will comfort her.
But help me, Lord,
   to lead her to someone who truly understands:
      to an objective, loving person
      who has the tools to pry apart the debris
      and find the meaning in all this problem.
   She needs such a person to love and direct her.
Help us both to find someone who can help her
   and to rely on you when troubles overwhelm us.

ON THE
DEATH
OF A
CHILD

Father, death is so huge,
and this tragedy is so terribly real to all of us.
I feel weak
    when I imagine the feelings of these parents
        who have lost their dear child.
I am grateful for your protection of my loved ones,
and I am longing to help these parents in their grief.
Please give them strength to see ahead, God.
Help them to trust in Jesus' victory over death.

Give them the comfort
  of tears
  and memories
  and the love of friends.
Bless us as we try to minister to them
  in the long days to follow.
And bless the little children everywhere:
  those living,
  those in eternity,
  and those in need of love and care.
Bless anyone who suffers under the sting of separation,
  the loneliness death brings to the living.
Truly, you are the only power in heaven and earth
  who can understand and see us through
    such deep sadness.

PEOPLE
ARE NOT
PICTURE
POSTCARDS

Lord, I get enmeshed in a first-glance life.
　　"Hmmm, she's awfully heavy these days."
　　"My! What a nice new coat."
　I busy my eyes with clothes and styles
　　　and the surface activities of another.
　I miss her smiles,
　　　the questions in her eyes,
　　　a wistful look.

I listen to overtures
  and miss the symphony of knowing persons.
I hear only the external sounds
  of the person talking.
I don't listen to her;
  I'm too busy plotting out my own next sentence.
I miss her hint for help,
  the sadness in her voice.
Help me to remember
  that people are not picture postcards.
People are beautiful, long, complex letters,
  waiting to be revealed and understood.
Make me a perceptive and sensitive reader, Lord,
  not preoccupied with first glances,
  but a scholar of human love.

BLESS
THIS POOR
MOTHER,
LORD

Jesus the children were eating a breakfast
   of bacon drippings and water.
My hands were full of groceries to give
   but my heart is wracked with sadness
   and discouragement at their plight.
Is it such a transgression to be divorced and poor?
Are we so callous
   that we resent helping this mother
     and these children?
   Do we begrudge them bacon drippings?
She cannot work now.
   The babies are small.
   Babysitters are expensive
   and there is no day care center.
   The rent is high.
   Her skills are few;
     she didn't expect to have to
     support a family some day.

She has no money to go to school.
No refrigerator,
poor heat,
and three days ago her welfare check
    was stolen.
I understand her defeated expression, Lord.
    She is a human;
        she feels discouraged and trapped.
    She loves her children;
        she wants to provide for them.
    She was embarrassed to have
        well-dressed strangers
        bringing eggs and milk.
    Grateful, but embarrassed.
I will carry her portrait with me all day—
    this mother
        and her two small children at breakfast.
I know you see her, Lord.
What do you want me to do?
    I can relieve *my* tension by just
        talking to you this way.
    But how do I relieve *her* burden?
How, Lord, do I best love those children
    and families like theirs?
Bless all poor mothers, Lord.
    Help me to help them in your name.

PRAYER FOR SINGLE PEOPLE

God, forgive me for being insensitive.
    I forgot she is single.
I'm so accustomed to relating to people in pairs.
Our culture is family centered.
Our lives are directed toward marriage:
    magazines glamorize weddings,
    advertisers imply that romance
        and marriage are expected,
    subtly and directly we separate the unmarried
        from ourselves
        in jokes and in patterns of entertainment
        or behavior.

Carelessly I spoke to her,
  condescendingly,
    pity in my voice.
  How cruel!
    I'm sorry, Lord.
I was eager to have her be "like us."
  How often we do that by playing matchmaker
    with half-willing friends.
  We have minimized the fulfillment,
    the rewards, and the contributions
    of a career woman,
    assuming homemaking is the most worthy
    profession.
  We question rather than accept
    a bachelor's choice of lifestyle.
    We tease and cajole
    and hint.
Help us be more fair, Lord.
  Help us recognize that all people
    have their humanity in common.
  No lifestyle is the only acceptable way.
Forgive my assuming, all-knowing manner
  toward this lovely lady.

THANK YOU
FOR THE
EVER-MOVING
SPIRIT

What a thoughtful gesture!
   A homemade coffee cake is like
      a breath of spring in the middle of February.
   And why she brought it, I don't know.
   She is such a nice person!
      It's a special day.

Lord, thank you for such lovely surprises in life.
But, you know, I forget to give credit
    in all the places where it is due.
When someone is thoughtful
    by bringing bakery treats
    or calling on a dreary day,
    by asking about my health
    or offering to help at just the right moment,
I usually am grateful for
    "such a nice person" in my life.
I forget that it is the impetus of God
    in the Holy Spirit which moves persons.
Thank you for the ever-moving Spirit
    which opens people to one another.
Thank you for your small moments of joy!

SEE
THE
UNMARRIED
MOTHER

Dear Jesus, see the unmarried mother.
   Bless her. Love her.
She feels alone in deep decision
She feels the dilemma of determining
   whether she is capable of raising her child alone
   or whether she should let others
     accept this opportunity for her.
She gets discouraged
   knowing the subtle and flagrant
     judgment of other persons,
   needing the sound advice of those
     who are objective and wise
   waiting, waiting. . . .unsure.

She lives in stark reality.
    The past is truly past for her.
    Today and the unknown tomorrow
        are her life now.
    The movement of a small one
        constantly reminds her
        of the irrevocable decision she must make.
Please Jesus, love her.
    Help her know what is best
        and to live with her resolution.
    Soothe her in moments of despair and fear
        and in her hours of labor and delivery.
    Give her warm friends and loved ones who care,
        people to be with her now
        and in the days to come.
    Give her dignity.
        She is a human being in need
        of tenderness and respect.
I pray for the unmarried mother—
    that she may be loved
        and understood
        and blessed.

THIS
FAMILY
NEEDS
YOU

O heavenly Father,
   watch them tonight.
   Hear their aching sighs,
     their prayers,
     their cries.
This family needs you.
They will not sleep well.
Their hours are so long now,
   so deranged in their confusion over their child
   as they share this overwhelming burden
   and attempt to love one another through it all.

Help them understand this storm of life.
   Give them the vision to see that this crisis
      can reaffirm your love for them
      and their love and support of one another.
Forgive us Lord, that we create and permit
   such sadness in lives.
      Make me responsive to their silent call.
Strengthen this family
   in the dark stillness of tonight,
   in the glaring truth of another day,
   in their deep need for you.

LOVE
THE
LITTLE
CHILDREN

I'm remembering a little boy, Jesus.
I was called to substitute teach in an inner city school.
    I came to a third grade class.
There had been a substitute trained for high school
    in the class the day before.
        The room was in a shambles.
One little boy had been quite naughty—
    just a mite of a boy,
        blond with sparkling eyes.
I liked him
    and he liked me, too.
Near the end of the day, we talked.
        All was not well at his home.

It was time to dismiss the class.
He took my arm,
    and I looked down into his serious eyes.
Quietly he said, "Will you please
    take me home with you?"
If he could have heard my thoughts,
    he would have heard me crying.
I could only say,
    "Oh I wish I could!"
Then he was gone, out the door.
How I wish. . . .
Jesus, wherever he is today,
    please bless him.
    Whatever his life is now,
        please help him.
        Please give him love.
    Protect this little boy who wanted me
        to take him home and love him.
Jesus, he is one of so many children in the world
    who need love and attention.
        Watch over them.
This is the kind of experience I need
    to be reminded of the core of life's meaning.
Thank you for taking me to the third graders,
    and Jesus,
        love the little children.

I AM
POSSESSIVE
LORD

I am possessive, Lord.
I speak in "mys":
    my children,
    my husband,
    my house,
    my garden,
    my church,
    my job,
    my life,
    my choice.
I try to keep my family exclusive to myself:
    I want the children with me when they visit
        from far away
    I want them home for the holidays;
    I want them with me
        when they have other activities
        to which they give priority;

I even want them to remain always young,
    dependent,
    needing me,
    and subject to my decisions.
I build a world with me in the center
    and mine carefully arranged around me,
        snug and secure.
I toy with creation,
    carelessly using and wasting living things
        as if they were mine alone.
Proud of achievements, I call them my own:
    beautiful roses,
    kind friends,
    sufficient income,
    talents or knowledge.
Quell my need to selfishly possess persons and things
    and all the creative world.
Make me less a leader
    and more a creature, being led
    and grateful for your multitude of gifts to me.
Thy will be done on earth
Thy kingdom come
Thine is the power and the glory.
    Remind me.

I NEED
SELF-DISCIPLINE,
LORD

If I really loved you, God,
    I would not overeat.
    I would not destroy me—
        my "me" which can serve you best
        when I am healthy.
    I would not destroy me
        if I really loved you.
If I really sought you,
    I would know that discipline and will power
        develop slowly,
        whether in diets or in faith.

I would discipline all my life
   if I really sought you.
I will change
     with your help,
   not because my clothes don't fit,
   nor because I feel uneasy when I feel uncontrolled,
   but because I care about you.
Restrain me in temptation.
   Strike down my selfish need
     to acquire
     to be powerful,
     to yield,
     to eat!
Give me the serenity I need
   to be assured that you love me
   so that I will want to take the best care
     of myself—my offering to you.

THANKS
FOR
TEARS

I can't stop crying, God.
   I simply cannot stop!
      It feels so good!
I've needed this release for a long time.
   I see it now.
I've been driving myself to accomplish
   and perform,
   and function,
      and I forgot to feel.

I've been like an empty liturgy until now.
Now I'm singing again,
    heart and, thank God, soul.
Your Holy Spirit has interceded, all right.
I might have gone on and on, struggling.
But you turned me around with a few gentle words
    from a kind friend,
and I've been feeling better ever since.
    Thanks for tears.

SEND ME
HOPEFUL
INTO
TOMORROW

O God, I dread tomorrow.
   What can it possibly bring?
   I would be a dreamer to hope for anything
      but a difficult day.
   Human relationships are not easy.
   Interplay with others can be
      a virtual nightmare.
   I cannot sleep, anticipating and wondering.

Jesus, don't let me shrink from tomorrow;
    difficulty is part of life too.
Make me instead a dreamer!
Make me hopeful
    for life is too rich to waste it on dread—
    the possibilities for good are too great
        to mire in worry and anxiety.
You were the divine dreamer
    of a world of peace
    and a humanity of unmatched kindness—
    of persons who trust their Father
        and love the life he gives us.
A glorious, possible, divine dream!
Make me a dreamer, Jesus,
    and send me hopeful
    into tomorrow.

THANKS
FOR
LISTENING

Forgive me, Lord, but I am frustrated by them.
   They do not listen to me!
They are so sure
   that experience is right
   and that my idealism is admirable
     but foolish.
Their years are unchallengeable.

But I've been taught to question everything:
    Is it liquid or vapor?
    Is it true or false?
    Is it reporting or editorializing?
    Is it fact or opinion?
        "Find the facts."
        "Don't guess."
        "Be sure."
        "Spell it out."
But they don't listen to my view.
They don't have to agree with me—
    just listen.
I'm glad you hear me anyway.
    Somebody has to give me my chance, too.
Thanks for listening.
        I'm not so upset anymore.

GIVE
ME
RESPONSE
ABILITY

Lord, it is hard to keep up to date.
Change moves so quickly
    that noon news is history by 6:00,
    and conflicting opinions flash at us
        in neon-sign rapidity.
Decisions are crucial:
    local elections,
    environmental protection,
    population growth and hunger,
    war, race, and school bond issues.
Sometimes I feel weighed down
    by the responsibility of citizenship
        in a chaotic, confused world.
I want to enclose myself in a hermitage,
    away from decisions and strife.

I have enough personal decisions to make
    without trying to carry the world on my shoulders.
O Lord, I hear you, I hear you.
    You say that I am called to respond
        not in apathy or retreat,
        but in vigorous concern.
    You do not ask me to carry all the weary world
        on my small shoulders,
        but to carry my portion of the load
so that no one else must bend to lift
        my shunned responsibility.
    You ask me to respond by being
        aware,
        willing to read,
        flexible,
        unafraid of change.
And you will stand by
    supportive and strong,
        never asking more of me than I am able,
        with your help, to endure.
I hear you Lord.
And because tomorrow is made better
    not by wishing
    and not by retreat
And because this world and its people belong to you,
    I am willing to participate in the world.
        Guide and help me

THANK
YOU
FOR
HEALTH

Heavenly Father,
    we are never appreciative enough of our health.
    we complain about head colds,
    and we indulge in self-pity.
But Lord,
    to be able to move about,
    to see,
    to eat normally,
    to sleep,
      is such a blessing!

Forgive our complaining, Lord.
Bless those who are truly sick
   who are confused in mental illness
   who are in sharp or gnawing pain
   who are afraid to die.
Strengthen us in our stewardship
   of bodies and emotions and minds
so that we enter robustly
   into a life which glorifies
      your creativity and your goodness.

LORD,
I AM
JEALOUS!

Lord, I am jealous!
   I am scheming and frightened—jealous.
   What a small feeling—powerful within me,
      yet not worthy of the energy of anyone!
I doubt.
I compete,
and I succumb to my fears
   of being outdone by another.
I calculate my activities around my jealous desire
   to equal another person's achievements
      or possessions
      or abilities.

In the process
   I stifle my own creativity,
   and I seek my glory rather than yours.
You are a jealous God.
You cannot allow me to substitute my gods—
   my stubborn pride
   my need to win
   my self esteem—
      for my dedication to you
      and my understanding of others.
So God, scrape away this weakness of mine.
Replace my mistrust with fire—
   a fire that burns in obedient devotion
   to the great,
      the jealous God.

KEEP
ME
GRATEFUL
AND GENEROUS

Oh Jesus!
 I have had a wonderful day!
 I so enjoy a new look in my house:
  rearranging the furniture
  or a little vase of daisies in a gray corner,
  or today—a whole new piece of furniture!
Help me keep this event in perspective, Jesus.
 Furniture and decorating are my toys.
 I can so easily be like a child,
  wanting more and more toys,
  making life a plaything.
  "Gimme, gimme, gimme."
Keep me grateful.
 Thank you for all the things I have.

And keep me generous and sensitive;
   my new bookcase could heat someone's cold hut,
   and my dollar in the offering plate yesterday
      was not a sacrificial gift;
      it was a token, a ritual.
   My dollar shouldn't be able to smother
      my caring for those who have only meager lives
And Jesus,
   Let me not think that I personally have earned
      this privilege of property.
   You made it all.
   You made this bounty available to me.
   I want to be responsible in my use of it.
Thank you for today,
   but thank you most of all for the gift of life—
      living!
May I use it gladly,
   responsibly,
    and fully
      for you.

EASE
MY
ACHE,
LORD

I am so terribly, terribly disappointed.
   God, it hurts!
My hopes have been shattered
   like a full bottle of milk,
   and I cannot bear to think
   of cleaning up after it all.
      It is easier to despair.
It is hard to imagine overcoming
   this bursitis of the spirit.

Why did I let myself hope like this?
Why did I dream of victory and joy?
Lord, it is because I know no other way
    than to hope.
        Hope is your whole scheme of life.
Because I am born to care,
    born to serve,
    born to hope,
        I will risk disappointment again.
But ease my ache, Lord.
    Ease the pain.

THANKS
FOR
BREAD

Father God, we are grateful for bread,
   for warm, brown beauty,
   fragrance and flavor,
   and the senses to appreciate them all.
Thank you for bounty, O God.
Thank you for enough!
   for hors d'ouvres and desserts
   for land not wearied by time,
     but for a land, new in the measure of your time,
     for fertile, productive earth given us to till.

God, remind us
    that bread is more than food for the body.
Bread in the stomach of a famished man
    can also restore hope to his emaciated soul:
    his hope that his child will not know
        a lifetime of hunger,
    his hope that his child can believe
        that we who live in plenty are not selfish,
        but loving human beings.
You have shared the gift of Christ with us.
Open our hearts to share our love
    and our bread—
        for Jesus' sake.

CAST
OUT
MY
FEAR

I am afraid, lying here alone.
    I am afraid of the dark!
    And I'm too proud to turn on a light.
        What am I, a child?
Yes, of course I am. I am a child.
    I cannot control all of the world around me
        any more than a child can.
    I need to feel protected too.

I am able to understand the world, though.
And I can understand that when my husband is gone,
   I am certain to feel insecure.
I can understand that I am lonely
      and that the quiet from the absence
         of his breathing and moving near me
         makes me more attuned
            to every sound of the house.
And I can understand that I am indeed
      just a child of God.
   I need the confidence of believing that you do
         watch over this world of ours.
      "Nestling bird nor star in heaven
      such a refuge e'er was given."
Send me your perfect love.
   Cast out my fear.

LOOK
AT
MY
FISTS!

Father, look at my fists—
    clenched tight!
I have been stewing all day over her conversation.
I rehash the words that have been exchanged,
    and what I wish I could say.
And now I have caught myself
    in a fit of revenge.

How I have deluded myself into thinking
   that revenge is something "uncivilized,"
but I have been scheming all day, haven't I?
Am I so easily bruised and so doggedly proud
   that I cannot turn my cheek?
Have I spent one moment
   putting the best construction on her acts,
   looking for a reason for her behavior?
"Vengeance is mine," says the Lord.
I had better let you take over this revenge
   for me, Lord,
      because it is consuming all that is loving in me.
         Forgive me.

GIVE ME YOUR PATIENCE, LORD

I need patience, Lord:
    patience with the growing of children
        who can be noisy and all-knowing,
        needing and late!
    patience with humanity
        who fails,
        rails,
        hurts,
        and ignores;

patience with myself—
  slow to change
  short with my family
  given to quiet hate and
  selfish;
patience with the mysteries of life—
  the unsearchable truths,
  the workings of justice,
  the development of soul,
  the Plan.
It is an everyday struggle
  which you understand
  and only you can ease.
Give me your patience, Lord.

DOES
EVERYONE
HAVE FAITH
EXCEPT ME?

O Lord, does everyone have faith except me?
   I watch them talk at Bible Study.
      They seem to imply faith is easy.
Lord! It's hard!
   I battle with disappointments;
   I neglect disciplined faith.
   I rationalize,
   I doubt,
   I criticize,
   I fail.
Am I really the only one who feels this way?
    or are we all ashamed to tell who we really are?
    Are we afraid other Christians won't forgive?

Help us accept our human bond, Lord:
    our need for one another's forgiveness,
    our bond of human frailty,
    our mutual struggles in faith,
    the joy of helping each other fight the good fight.
Free us from our pride
    so that we may ask for help from one another.
Help us trust that other Christians will understand
    our weaknesses and troubles,
      because they too are Christians.
    We will reaffirm your power
      when we acknowledge our deficiency.
    We will be inspired
      as we help one another through difficulties,
      through distress to victory.
Help all of us
    to share our whole selves,
    so that we experience in the midst of failure
      a community of forgiven persons,
      alive with our shared faith!

BLESS THE CHURCH SCHOOL TEACHERS

Heavenly Father,
　　being a Sunday school teacher is a capsule of life.
Few of us feel adequate,
　　yet all of us feel, in some way, called.
　　We may not define our call, yet we respond
　　　　because children need direction,
　　　　because we may be capable of teaching,
　　　　because our particular church needs us,
　　　　because you asked.

We appreciate the guidance and learning materials
   of skilled people.
We ask forgiveness when we do not appropriate
   enough time for preparation.
Let us listen well to the young,
   learning from them as well as leading them.
And we ask that you send the Spirit
   to lead us in this ministry,
      for we need inspiration,
      and most of all,
      we need patience and love.
It is your love shining through us
   in our relationships with children
   that will be the most valuable lesson,
   for your greatest command and gift is love.
      Guide us Father.

SUMMER
FAITH

This is a paper plate day!
I fill my plate with potato chips and hot dogs,
   with the sound of crickets
   and the joy of children reveling in summer.
How convenient to have this disposable plate—
   no dishes, more sun-time.
I wonder, is mine also a paper plate faith—
   disposable in nice weather,
   quick and easy,
   emergency relief?

Do I meditate during Lent
    and run free all summer,
        basking in God's sun
        and behaving as if it were my own?
Do I covet the fragrances of sentimental holidays—
    joyous Easter and quiet Christmas—
        enjoying the perennial favorites
        with little gardening of my soul in between?
Give me more perseverance than that, Lord.
    I need more than beaches and sun worship.
    I need some sand in my character, too.

ONE LORD, ONE FAITH, ONE BIRTH

You did not divide us into denominations, Lord.
They have come because of man—
 his variety of needs and responses,
 his fallibility,
 his need to change and re-form,
  and to change again.
Most of us get thrown into a denominational
   category,
 and we develop with it,
 grow to love it,
 and never discover that we could also appreciate
  something else

Heavenly Father, we need to be more open.
    Are there Christian truths we have not been
        willing to share with one another?
    Are there persons we have not known
        because we are secluded
        in our own private grottos of faith?
    Are we prepared to change—
        not in our faith—but in our interpretation
        and expression of Christian truths?
Help us to sing with conviction:
    one lord,
    one faith,
    one birth.
Unite your Christian community
    in a common servanthood to mankind,
    a common declaration of the love of God
        in Jesus Christ.

I AM
LOVED
REGARDLESS

Lord, I've hardly accomplished a thing today.
　　What a waste!
　　　　About all I've done is the dishes.
Oh! I'm slipping into that old trap again
　　measuring my value
　　　　　in terms of work accomplished.
　　　　"Busy busy busy.
　　　　Fill every minute with tasks.
　　　　Relaxation is evil.
　　　　The best man is the hard-working man.
　　　　Labor is more virtuous than art or recreation."
What a dilemma I would find myself in
　　if suddenly I was unable to work.
　　　　How would I justify my existence?

Is that what I am doing these days:
    participating just to feel I'm doing
        something—anything—
        as long as I'm active?
Jesus does not measure me in terms
    of financial success,
    or a day's work for a day's wages,
    or whether I have finished all the jobs
        on my list of things to do.
He loves me
    when I'm resting,
    when I'm learning,
    when I'm working,
    when I fail,
    when I can no longer market my abilities
        to society.

I may not have failed today.
    But if I have,
        I am loved regardless.

MAKE
WORSHIP,
WORSHIP

Heavenly Father,
    make worship more than routine
    make worship, *worship:*
        gratitude for living,
        confession of feeling,
        adoration of power,
        worship.
Perhaps Lord,
I sometimes require
    new ways of expressing our time-tested needs—
    new liturgies,
    new hymns.
I need to plan for enough rest Saturday night
    to make me alert on Sunday morning.

I get careless, Lord,
    singing familiar hymns,
    hearing what I choose to hear in
        spot-dash attention to the Word
    treating worship like
        "a good way to start the week" or
        "a place to get a good thought for the day."
Give the conviction that worship is me—giving.
Worship is giving
    my thoughts to you,
    my burdens and needs to you,
    my dedication to you
        for more than today or for this week.
Develop in me a consistent, committed attitude
    toward worship,
    where I am awake to the happenings
        of Christian faith in my life,
    where I continue to grow and change
        in my relationship to you
        forever.

GOOD
IN
EVERYTHING

Dear Lord, life is very full and interesting.
Your guidance is revealed in unexpected ways.
   Today I heard you in a soap opera.
I've often scolded myself for watching that program.
   It isn't always real.

No single family experiences so many traumas,
    even if the difficulties do reflect our society.
The acting is not always good,
    and the episodes are drawn out to keep
    me watching the story—and the ads.
But today, on that program, I finally heard
    you in the person of a young woman.
Preachers had said it
    and friends
    and leaders wiser than I.
But I *heard* the woman on television.
She told me what you have always ordained:
    that even the worst experiences
        even the damaging influences of our lives
    are to be remembered and credited.
I am more a person in every experience,
    as I grow from what I learn.
I need not deny myself—
    my disappointments, my failures, my past.
Even suffering is good.
My only imperative is to grow—
    to recognize who I am and where I'm going,
to learn—even from the absence of love—
    what it is to love.
Thank you for revealing this important aspect of life
    in my soap opera.

I AM
YOUR
TEMPLE,
LORD

I am your temple, Lord—
    I, whatever corner I stand on.
I left my dedication to you in church last Sunday.
I left you like so much dust
    in the carpet threads of the center aisle,
and I trampled mankind all week long.
    Forgive me.
Hymnals,
pianos,
carpets and pews.
And you Lord?
    Is that really you in the wood cross
        and the stained glass
        and the portrait on the wall?
Or are you in this temple
    that I wear every day
    out in the winds of discontent
    out in the rain of unhappy lives
    and the sunlight of love that shows?
You are stirring inside me, Lord.
    My well-trimmed heartless walls are cracking,
        the light is coming through!
Your temple is on the move!
    Send me, Lord!
        Send me.

C20672

Mattison, Judith N
    Prayers from a woman's heart [by] Judith Matt
Illus. by Audrey F. Teeple. Minneapolis, Augsburg
House [1972]

    96 p. 21 cm. $3.50

2 2/89

2 4/09

    I. Title.

PS3563.A86P7   811'.5'4
ISBN 0-8066-1219-3

Library of Congress   72 [4]

72–